CAPTIVATED

ALSO BY MICHAEL CERVAS

Inside the Box (poems, 2007)

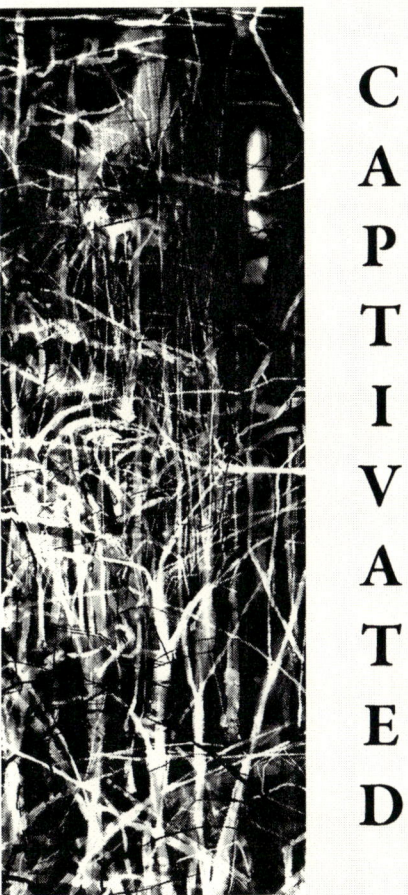

CAPTIVATED

Poems by

Michael Cervas

Michael Cervas

Antrim House, Simsbury, Connecticut

Library of Congress Control Number: 2011928385

ISBN: 978-1-936482-04-7

Printed & bound by United Graphics, Inc.

First Edition, 2011

Front cover painting ("Treescape") by Bryan Nash Gill

Author photograph by Richard Bergen

Book design by Rennie McQuilkin

Antrim House
860.217.0023
AntrimHouse@comcast.net
www.AntrimHouseBooks.com
21 Goodrich Road, Simsbury, CT 06070

for Josh, Emily Autumn, and Anne

ACKNOWLEDGEMENTS

Thanks to Kate Caspar, Brian Ford, and Bob Voorhees, who have read many drafts of these poems; to my students and colleagues, who have listened to different versions of them; and to my wife Deb, who has lived through all of them with me.

The author would like to acknowledge the following journals in which several of these poems first appeared, sometimes in slightly altered forms:

The Bulletin: "Falling in Love"
The Cape Rock: "Skin"

Thanks also to Bryan Nash Gill, whose painting "Treescape" is featured on the cover and inside pages of this book, and to Ken Mason, who photographed the painting.

Publication of this book would not have been possible without the generous support of Westminster School and the Ford-Goldfarb Fund. So special thanks to Kirsten Ford and Maureen Goldfarb.

TABLE OF CONTENTS

I. PITCHING AND CATCHING

II. HERE ON EARTH

III. MEETING MR. BUDDHA

IV. JOURNEYS

V. LOVE LOVE

Captivated: *1. orig., being taken or held captive or prisoner; 2. having one's attention or affection captured, as by beauty or love; 3. filled with wonder or delight*

PITCHING
AND
CATCHING

Eating in Eden

If a boy wanted something to eat
on a summer's morning in the woods
behind our house on Thorn Drive
— something sweet and cold —
he had only two choices really.
He could shinny up the thick trunk
of the ancient black cherry tree
in the very middle of our forest,
inch himself out precariously
along the ever-narrowing branches,
then reach up to grab the wine-
dark cherries floating in the sky,
pop them by handfuls into his mouth
and spray the pits out in a juicy rain.

Or he could squirrel his way deep
into the center of the wild blackberries
that hugged the ridge at the border
of the woods and the old farmer's land,
risking scratches and skinned elbows
to tunnel far enough into the dark canopy
of bushes to find the ripest ones,
thimbles that stained his fingers and face
with wild splotches of mulberry paint
and soaked into his shorts so deeply
he could smell the berries' tartness
fermenting there even months later.

Either place, up high and suspended
above the forest's carpet of loam
or lying down low on the soft ground
in the silence of the aromatic earth,
a boy felt alone, safe and scared.

What the Nuns Taught Me

I knew it would happen like this —
the nuns of St. Aloysuis taught me well:
every little pleasure is really a tiny sin,
the greater the pleasure, the greater the sin,
and you always pay for your sins,
little and big, in this world and the next.
So just last week when twenty-two
of the twenty-eight shots I took swished
through the net in my Monday night
basketball game, even though at 53
I was over a decade older than anyone else
on the floor, and again when I won
every last game I played at Wednesday
night squash, even against opponents
who usually clobber me, I knew that soon
I would have to pay.

So when I started feeling a tingling
in my fingers, a tiny numbness creeping
up my right arm by the weekend,
I figured it was only the beginning,
and I remembered standing outside
St. Aloysuis School on the playground
as snow like flecks of tissue paper
swirled in the bitter air of early March,
liberated by some hardened 8th graders
to scurry around telling the little kids
the nuns had cancelled school for the day,
feeling so free and so powerful until
I ran smack into Sister Wilbert,
the notorious scourge of the 6th grade.

I can still feel the lash of her hand
against my cheek, my eyes erupting
in tears.

        It's a good thing, I suppose,
that this Monday every shot I launched,
no matter how smoothly the ball rolled
off my fingers, bounced harmlessly away.

Truck Farm

The summer I was thirteen
I got my first job on a truck farm,
35 cents an hour, 10 hours a day, 6 days a week.
I liked sitting in a circle bunching scallions,
hated being bent over, weeding rows of chard,
watched surreptitiously as an old migrant named Joe
turned his head sideways and blew a line of snot
out of each of his nostrils, even got to ride in
with the boss to Farmers Market once or twice,
but spent most of my time day-dreaming about girls
and worrying about you, pregnant at 41.
I didn't know much then, only that older mothers
were *at risk* — I was afraid you would die in childbirth.
I never even thought about the little girl
you were ready to die to have at last,
after four boys, the fruit of all
that work and fear.

Dreaming

"I never dream at all," the boy says in class,
but all I remember is how hard I dreamed back
when I was sixteen, dribbling on the asphalt
court my father had made, wearing gloves
in the icy weather, pretending I was Havlicek,
draining as many baseline jumpers as I could,
especially from the right side because whenever
I missed, the ball would bound all the way
down the hill into the dense brush,

and later dreaming I was Bobby, his voice
the clear bell of justice itself, his eyes on fire,
his hands chopping through the morass
of discarded promises and dreams deferred,
every night our voices raised together in protest,
crying for that newer better world no matter
what the cost, no matter how many widows
would be left draped in black standing
all alone in the freezing rain.

Pitching and Catching

So I'm sauntering across
the quad on a hot summer's day
going to check on the mail

when I glance down the road
and see two roofers, one perched
right on top of the gymnasium,

poised like a weathervane,
the other just stepping out of his van
suddenly pitching something,

a 95 mph fastball, almost invisible,
right at his partner, who flashes
out his left hand and snags the object

(hammer? stapler? cold drink?)
right out of mid-air. "Nice toss," I shout,
not knowing whether they'll even

hear me. A moment of grace
in the rush of time. "Hey, what about
the catch?" cries the other guy

catching me by surprise. "Great
catch too," I yell, as all of us laugh
and I remember quiet evenings

long ago when I played pitch
and catch with my father, and later
with my son, a game as ancient

as our species, the way we come
to know each other in the day-to-day
pitching and catching of our lives.

To My Younger Self

Yesterday, in a desperate attempt
      to find my brother's e-mail address —
I was late as always in sending out
      birthday wishes — I punched his name
into *Google* and dozens of sites
      floated up, some with his name,
others with the names of others
      I knew, another brother, my wife,
even a few nieces I didn't know I had,
      and, of course, my own name too
appearing quite often actually. But
      looked at closer the Michael Cervas
I was reading about couldn't be me.
      These links were to newspapers
from Fort Osage, to sports articles
      about high school cross-country races.
This Michael Cervas seems to be
      a seventeen-year-old boy, running
great times (at least by my standards) —
      18:56 in the Kansas City Metro.
So here I am, thinking the dark
      thoughts of a fifty-two-year-old man
while my alter ego is busy navigating
      the halls of high school, pulling his hair out
over impossible calculus problems
      (the hair I no longer have), getting
up the nerve to ask Lauren or Liz
      to go with him to the prom, hanging out
on Friday nights with his friends,
      shooting baskets on lonely Saturdays
in a gym whose shafts of sunlight
      take me, even now, all the way back

to North Catholic High School
       in the winter of 1964 where a skinny
Michael Cervas, hoping to make
       the JV team, once shot 250 foul shots
then headed off to the locker room
       for a shower before hitch-hiking home.
It's funny — I always thought that if
       I had a chance to do it all over again,
if I were whisked magically back
       to high school, I would do so many
things differently. I'd be so much
       wiser about girls, I'd avoid so many
of the traps of adolescence, I'd know
       all the tricks about just what to say
to my friends and enemies, I'd know
       just how to maneuver through all
those crowded hallways of the world.
       But now that I finally have the chance
to speak the truth to a younger me,
       I'm afraid I don't have much to offer.
So, to the young Michael Cervas
       in Fort Osage — my chance at a do-over —
I say only, *Keep on running, I hope*
       the wind will always be at your back.
I think I'll let you figure out the rest
       on your own. The mistakes you make
will blaze the pathways of your life,
       and that's exactly the point after all:
it wouldn't be your destiny if you
       weren't the one working it out.
So go on, run past rivers and fields,
       lose yourself in your runner's dreams,
but keep your eyes on the distant stars,
       your feet, light and sure, on the ground.

Hope

There's hope
for the girl after all,
my teenaged daughter,
the one who sneaks away
from physics problems
to watch *What Not to Wear,*

but who tonight I find
hunched over a small tower
of albums she's retrieved
from the crate in our basement,

lost in *Abbey Road* and *Blue,*
wound up in *Tapestry,* studying
the liner notes like a poem,
listening beyond the scratches,
telling us records are better,
much more real.

The Theory of Relativity

I've always loved the way
the world opens with song each day
even before there's any light,
the birds pulling those first rays
out of the pillow of night
note by note, soloists in flight,
trading two's and four's, trilling away
until the whole band's got it right

and I am wide awake,

                but

tonight at the dinner table
my wife and daughter sit and chat
about the awful racket that snaps their cable
of sleep well before daybreak and that
drives them crazy. In fact, if they were able,
they agree, they'd grab a baseball bat,
drive the songsters into a stable,
beat them dead, and that would be that!

HERE ON EARTH

Loss

Loss takes up inside of everything sooner or later and eats
right through it.   — Sue Monk Kidd

I lost the only watch my mother ever gave to me
— a graduation present — on a summer's day

at an *Eat 'n Park* out by the Pennsylvania Turnpike.
I must've slipped it off in the bathroom to wash

my hands, and then left it there on the filthy sink.
Today, just a couple of days before the start of spring,

the persistent March sun is eating at the snow,
imperceptibly transforming all of winter's darkness

into pearly trickles of light. Just the same I know
there is darkness here too, ready to devour that sun.

My father was sitting at his desk, just after lunch,
looking at travel brochures, maybe dreaming

of the marble Aegean Sea, its mirror of blue
reflecting Athena's temple in the splashing sunlight,

when he clutched his chest and dropped out of my life.
One night when I was twelve, I awoke in a sweat,

tiptoed into the bathroom, turned on the light,
opened my mouth, and squinted hard at the mirror

to see bones and flesh crumbling away, like a photograph
dissolving in chemicals, until only my eyes were left.

Once, we lost our two-year-old on an idyllic morning
at one of her sister's games: all the other moms and dads

went to search with us in the suddenly labyrinthine
woods behind the fields, while all I could hear

was the cry of an invisible plane somewhere above.
Loss takes up inside everything sooner or later

and eats right through it. The planet spins, the galaxies
whirl, the infant stumbles into old age: why just last summer

I took an enormous branch from the oak in my yard —
eaten away inside by insects — and snapped it like a twig.

Journey to Aegina

for my Father

I thought I saw you there, leaning
against the railing, staring at all those
imposing yachts bobbing in the sun-
splashed waters of the Aegean Sea
on Christmas Eve as we waited for
the ferry from Piraeus to Aegina —
sleek yachts bound for Mykonos,
Naxos, and Crete — islands of pleasure
with their stuccoed houses chiseled
into white cliffs dotted with lemon trees
above the sparkling Mediterranean —
or maybe even Ithaca with its air
of suspended time, donkeys clomping
along cobblestone streets, fishing
boats with far-flung eyes painted
on their bows floating in the harbors.
Were you thinking of the triremes
loaded with oil and arms the day before
the soldiers set sail for ancient Troy?
Were you thinking of your own father
hiking through the hills of Macedonia
on his crooked way to Ellis Island?
When I looked again you were hobbling,
cane in hand, towards the harbor town.

Our ferry looped out into the bay,
then sliced through the narrow channel
between the Peloponnesian shores

and the first island away from Athens.
I heard your voice, for a moment —
oracular, mythic, the voice of a bard —
as we rounded the cape and entered
another world, the wine dark sea,
the sheltered hills, the cries of heroes
echoing in the sudden icy silence —
your words of invocation: *Sing to me,
my Muse, of the travels of Odysseus,
the man of twists and turns.* And
I thought of how you'd never make it back
from the land of shrouded darkness.
What would I say to you anyhow
if you turned and stepped towards me?
But you disappeared instead into the mists
of another anonymous seaside café.

Once again, after a bumpy bus ride
to the eastern edge of the island,
past teeming groves of pomegranates
and fields of ripening pistachios,
little stone huts carved into the hills,
retreats for the monks, reliquaries
of two dead or dying civilizations,
I sensed you alive still in the ruins
of the temple of Aphaia. We were
the only ones there on that holy day.
The children explored the collapsed
pillars, the secret entrances, while I
sat and listened for your hexameters
of gold, the comfort of your voice,
what I've been missing now for years.

Still everywhere I looked I saw only
the faces of my children, your children
too, whose eyes reflected the sunlight
off the sea, all the history I need to know
now all I know of you is truly gone.

On Marconi Beach

We're here at Marconi Beach
on a sunny day in June. The season
hasn't even started yet — no fees
for parking, no lifeguards on duty —
but still we see three or four dozen
spread out along the gleaming shingle
and a handful of children and teens
bravely wading into the freezing water,
an iciness no amount of sunshine
can ever begin to transform.

After we find a smooth spot
somewhere above the high tide line,
we lay out an old Indian blanket
and I whisper to my fifteen-year-old,
"Well, at least nobody's out too
far or in too deep today." She smiles
back knowingly at me, says "Thanks,
Mr. Frost, for that brilliant insight,"
grabs her friend and two boogie boards,
and heads straight for the arctic sea.

I sit down to finish McEwan's
On Chesil Beach, maybe the saddest
book I've ever read, and suddenly
I realize that all of us are out farther
and in deeper than we can ever know.
Like the girl we passed on our way,
shawled in black, huddled at the bottom
of the stairs, furiously scribbling

in her notebook, a million miles away
from anyone, a spot on the dunes.

Or the chirping twenty-somethings
behind us, on the day after the wedding,
full of gawking bravado and secret
fears, their own marriages floating off
in the dangerous, hazy distance.
Or the little chubby boy who watches
my daughter and her friend juggling balls,
passing them back and forth, looking
at last for his mother or father, panic just
starting to settle in as the very faintest
signals become roaring waves.

Anonymity

People disappear all the time:
alpine climbers gone in sudden falls

or lonely swimmers bobbing
in water so serene it looks like sky

just going under one moment
for good — not a trace left behind,

or children in Sudanese villages
ripped from their beds by the dark —

families, tribes, nations, all stolen
from history, untranslatable,

like my Aunt Grayce who held me
in her elastic arms so long ago

lost in the middle of a Florida night
in the seamless arc of anonymity.

Driving Home from the DMV
I Discover the Basic Operating
Principle of the Universe

Driving home from the DMV
on a rainy afternoon

(actually my daughter is driving,
having just passed her test)

I glance over at what used to be
a gift shop with a cute

little luncheonette to discover
matching signs for two new places:

AVON DRIVING SCHOOL
and *TEENAGE WASTELAND*

revealing to all who have eyes
to see that irony is

the basic operating principle
of the universe.

Sun and Moon and Stars

An ordinary rainy winter's day
turned stormy in a moment

and the winds came thrashing
through the breezeway,

tearing apart the weathered
sun-and-moon-and-stars chime

that had dangled there for years.
I brought the pieces inside,

tried to patch them together again
with kite string and patience,

but the sun's rays were twisted
and the globe in the center was gone,

vanished — maybe forever!
Only here do winds like these

betray us with their sudden
unpredictabilities.

The moon itself makes no wind:
a footprint there will last a billion years

before infinitesimal fragments
lost from wandering micro-meteorites

fill up the depression with dust
and wipe away that image —

enough time, at least, to consider
the next step, not the way

it is here on earth where winds hurl
us from one moment to the next.

Skin

Right in the middle
of play, you stop to show me
the nearly invisible line
on your arm, precisely where
the cancer reappeared
one day almost two years
after that first surgery,

your face reddened now,
perspiration masking
your words, the slim odds
hanging like a ghost
over the court's shininess.
You hit every ball today
as though it were your last.

Absence

Like the purple scar carved
deep in the night's sky
by the sudden flash
of a shooting star
your absence
stays with
me for
ever.

And Some Time Later

It all looked so promising to you then,
after so many years of despair and poverty
in the Big Woods, now that someone had
actually spotted an Ivory-Billed Woodpecker

shrieking across Cache Lake, resurrected
from extinction, a miracle for everyone to see!
The God Bird will save us, you thought,
its delicate bill dropping dollars on little towns

and spare homes alike. And, at first,
with all those TV reporters and scientists
swarming into Arkansas like insects,
folks couldn't imagine even keeping up

with the hunger for Ivory-Billed hamburgers
and hand-carved, hand-painted replicas,
T-shirts emblazoned with the dazzling photo-
shopped images of the bird in all its glory.

And so you scraped together everything
you had, rented a little store on Main Street
and went into the hat-selling business,
sold $12,000 worth in the first three months

alone, but now, only two years later,
the streets are empty again. There've been
a few other sightings — apocryphal —
but still no incontrovertible photographs,

no homemade videos, no proof positive
that extinction is a lie — that entropy
can be reversed — and so, some time later,
you decide to throw away those boxes

of God Bird caps lying in the back room,
unopened, saturated with humidity,
while your husband — he spends all his days
in a rowboat, a camera on his lap.

Meeting Mister Buddha at the Doctor's Office

After making eye contact with Carol the receptionist
I sat down in a chair next to the only other person
in the office at the time. He seemed to be about
my age but he was pretty flabby (clearly he had not
played two and a half hours of tennis that morning
in the hot September sun). After a moment's silence,
Carol looked at the man and said, "Mister Buddha,
are you sure you don't have any cards with you?"
I looked up in surprise. You just never know when
or where the Buddha will appear, that's the truth.
He reckoned his wife must have taken the new ones,
and so there he was caught in a bureaucratic pickle.
But Carol — as always the mindful receptionist —
suggested he could just fax in the information later.
She asked him to fill out a registration form —
name and telephone number only. Mister Buddha
agreed there was no need for any more work
than was absolutely necessary, and then she asked
for his $15 co-pay, which he paid in small bills
before turning with a smile and heading out the door.
Suddenly I wasn't all that worried about my lab
results — and, in fact, they turned out to be just fine.
It was somehow good to know that Mister Buddha
himself doesn't always carry his insurance cards
and that he has a higher co-pay than I do.

Desire

"No freebies for the high rollers here,
no upgrades ever," whispers the manager,
holding her Manolo Blahniks daintily
as she leads her visitors into the sparkling
marble vestibule.
                    If you want to spend a night
in the penthouse suite — the entire 52nd floor —
of the new ultra chic Four Seasons Hotel,
you'll have to pony up the whole $30,000.

The spread, of course, is magnificent,
the decor beyond sumptuous, and it seems
there's no shortage of dreamers or fools
who want whatever notoriety or rush
comes along with tossing away thirty grand
for a room with *four* views

                    all for a single night
in a palace posh with sensuous amenities,
a radiant temple to conspicuous consumption
here where all the material boys and girls
shop, of course, at stores innocently named
Material Possessions.

                    And there in the hallway
sitting in the dazzle of a cut glass chandelier
on a teak table, a chiseled gold Buddha
watches over everything, his eyes wide open,
gone away and then come back again
to this very apotheosis of desire.

Asking for Let

It should be so simple,
the space being so confined,
and the probability of bodies colliding
so real, to raise your racquet,
stop everything, and say "Let, please,"

but in the game's frenzy,
the point is often decided before
the words can even escape
your mouth, leaving you fuming
over your costly reticence.

Or, really, did you continue
to play on because some little part
of you thought that if you had gotten
to the ball, you'd've won that point,
no need for politeness after all?

Excuses

They are always there, of course,
      turning this glinting morning forever
            into gray afternoon while I drift even

further from the next line for a poem:
      e-mails long left floating on the desktop,
            the new anthology I promised to preview,

planting annuals, Red Dianthus maybe,
      where the yellowed remnants of tulips lie,
            feeding the lazy cats, folding the laundry,

remembering the names of all the people
      no longer in my life today so that my life
            doesn't dry up and become an empty desert,

while my youngest mopes around the house,
      flitting from piano to books and back again,
            and finally into the study where she asks me

to make her a tunafish sandwich for lunch,
      which, of course, I say I'll do, and closing
            my eyes for an instant, sigh, and push SAVE.

In the Middle

of things is a comfortable place
to be: it's true you're often jostled,

pushed, pulled and spun around,
but at least you're not alone,

not wandering all by yourself
at the edges, maybe even slipping

across some forbidden border
to be cut off (forever? you wonder)

from the invariably convenient
tribes. No it's better to be

in the very center of the picture,
blurred and homogenized,

following the middle path, safe
from alienation's blows,

never at rest, never going
anywhere at all.

JOURNEYS

Delphi

1.

Millions of olive trees,
        green waves in a valley that rushes
                toward the invisible Gulf of Corinth,
a sky so distant it hurts to look up,
        the sunlight falling through the town
                splashing on the desecrated temples,
diffused now and oracular,
        on crooked paths of hardened dirt
                and broken pebbles, on stone slabs
stacked one against another
        scattered all along the Sacred Way,
                on Apollo's temple and Dionysos' theater
backed against the inscrutable
        opaque cliffs of Mount Parnassos,
                on the cleft rocks of Delphi's gorge.
The small modern town,
        removed over a century ago
                from amidst the rediscovered ruins,
whispers its dark secrets
        in the glowing light of evening,
                while the ancient site still holds
the final emptiness of night,
        and spills its wild seed madly
                down the always concupiscent valley.

2.

I can almost see her now,
the delicate priestess
swaying there on her tripod,
swooning in a narcotic spray
above the awful cauldron,
as I lean forward a little
to hear her mumbled words
but remember suddenly
that it was in fact the priests
who fashioned all the answers,
collected all the money,
controlling the trade routes,
creating and destroying
for over six hundred years.

Now the only music is
birdsong, unseen voices
teasing me up the chipped
and broken granite steps
to a narrow dirt path
overgrown with primroses
near the magic spring.

After the little girls
have been sent to bed
the languid women,
their soft dresses flowing
in night's warm breezes,
stroll along the street,
looking in the light

that frames the windows
of quaint boutiques
at earrings and bracelets
that glitter even now
as they once sparkled
thousands of years ago.

The only way
to arrive here today
at the very
center of the earth
is to follow
the narrow winding
road that curves
and scratches
up the steep walls
of the valley
toward the sacred
mountain,

the omphalos,
the navel of the world,
the void.

3.

As children climb the ragged hill to the stadium
where they race in laughter
across the fields,

I pause to rest beside the windswept theater
and wander over to the awful chasm that leads
to the Kastalian Spring.

Gaia, mother of the gods, was the first to sit here
beneath the mountain's clouds,
the first diviner, succeeded by her daughter Themis,
the granter of holy justice,
then by another daughter, the Titaness Phoebe,
who gave Apollo his famous surname
as a birthday gift.

Apollo himself built this very temple
after slaying the fearful serpent near a spring.
But why here?

This is the very place where the first two eagles
Zeus let fly from the ends of space
to find the center of the earth
met beside the cleft rocks above the sacred spring.

So Apollo's sanctuary housed the great omphalos,
and egg-like offerings were scattered
everywhere.

Silly stuff, I know, sheer myths,
stories for children.

4.

But when I stand here
        above the wild valley lolling
                beneath the mysterious mountain,
the sun sings out in air
        so clairvoyant I can sense
                I am standing on holy ground.
I can still hear
        those dancing waters
                leaping from the spring,
the same waters
        the priestess bathed in,
                maybe the same waters
the happy children
        will swim in tonight
                at the hotel in the quiet town.
Suddenly all of time
        telescopes into this
                one breathing moment
of sunlight and life
        as the world rushes
                out and in all at once
and everything
        that ever was
                appears and disappears.

Journeys

The only true voyage of discovery is not to
go to new places but to have other eyes.
　　　　　　　　 – Marcel Proust

It was a simple plan, really:
just slip a Chinese lama
across the border into Tibet
with a native surveyor, a *pundit,*
disguised as his manservant,
have them follow the Tsangpo
as far downstream as possible,
then toss 500 logs into the river.
If a group of British watchers
saw those same logs emerge
in the Brahmaputra, then indeed
a river did bisect those mountains
— impossible as that seemed —
cascading through some as-yet
unseen gorge.
　　　　　But the lama dawdled
for almost a year, drinking himself
from one tiny village to the next,
finally selling his servant Kinthup
to a headman and disappearing.
Kinthup labored as a slave there
for eleven months before escaping
to Marpung and the refuge
of a monastery.
　　　　　Four months later
the new monk sought permission
to go on a pilgrimage near where

the Tsangpo skirted the highest
of the peaks. At night he cut logs
from a forest and hid them all
in a cave. On a second pilgrimage
two months afterwards, he dropped
the logs, fifty a day for ten days,
into the fast-flowing Tsangpo,
working single-mindedly before
making his way home.
            The watch
on the Brahmaputra, of course,
had long since been abandoned,
so no one saw those little boats
floating dutifully down the water,
and Kinthup, unrewarded, lived
out his life as a simple tailor
in Darjeeling.
            His discovery
was subsequently found to be true:
the Tsangpo and the Brahmaputra
are indeed the same river. Still
what Kinthup saw with the eyes
of a slave in the deep shadows
of the highest, starkest Himalayas,
then alone in the starlit forest
with the eyes of a Tibetan monk
was the true end of all journeys.

Their Courage Too

You can say what you will about them,
their shify dealings with the natives,
their greed and rapacity, their penchant

for interminable, picayune doctrinal disputes,
but one thing's for certain: it took courage
to go to sleep at night in those scattered cabins

on the meadowlands, surrounded always
by the densest of forests, the specter
of bear and Indian as ineluctable and real

as the sound of the river's rushing,
the chirrs of crickets, the snapping of twigs.
They knew this new world could swallow

you whole in a moment's carelessness,
the silent wind sneaking down the mountain,
and you'd be gone for years or forever.

Like Daniel Hayes, 22, in the fall of 1707
rising at an early hour, bridle in hand,
to look for his missing horse in the woods

west of Salmon Brook, suddenly seized
by three Indians, compelled into captivity,
gone utterly for more than seven years,

or like Abigail Williams, mother of five,
climbing into her bed in the winter of 1680
after saying prayers with the children,

the candle's afterlight shimmering for only
a moment before she surrendered
— once again — to the night's embrace.

The Darkest Hour

Just before the sun sets
or just before the break of day
the sky will be very bright
but the road, the road will be dark,

says the irrepressible narrator
of a shopworn video for school teachers
who have to drive buses or vans
(designed to make us all safer drivers)

and I think, out of my almost sleep,
yes, that's the way it is,
the way it was for Saul unhorsed
in the dim twilight at Tarsus

suddenly so blinded by the slanting
fire flashing from the clouds
he had to crawl on his hands and knees
to find the invisible Roman stones,

or for Genghis, baffled and alone,
squinting out from his mountain cave
through waves of light lifting
off the rivers and filling the skies,

staring at seamless steppes
spilling into the unseen blankness
of history itself, or for me too
the very moment when we first met,

the flicker of the tiny candle
casting a circle of orange firelight
on the ceiling, our fingers
just barely touching on the tabletop,

not knowing whether this was
the beginning or the end,
lost in the night, afraid to take
even the very first step.

Hand In Hand Out

Who even knew what it meant,
each game beginning
at *love love* and staying there
sometimes forever,
it seemed, the partners dancing
into every corner
in a slow, exhausting march
of mysterious points
(but only when the server's tricks
worked and the ball
was *down* or *up,* not *in* or *out*).

You needed heart
to play such a guileful game
hand in hand out.
No wonder it's all about points
now, no romance,
no time for sweet imagining,
a point a rally,
every play ending in a score,
fast and ineluctable,
without the lovely give and take
of hand in hand out.

Falling in Love

How did they choose their subjects,
those sly Italian scientists at Pavia University
studying the mysterious *love molecule* —
known officially as Nerve Growth Factor (NGF)?
Did they put an ad in the local newspaper for
volunteers already stupefied by love's first pulls and tugs
to mosey on down to the lab
as soon as they started feeling the symptoms
(pitter-pattering heart, sweaty palms, giddiness)
or did they do a little scientific matchmaking of their own
in the nooks and crannies of their brightly lit laboratory
— where else would the chemistry be better, really?
Or maybe they set up a few spy-cams out on the piazza
trying to identify strangers with the telltale signs —
that light-footedness that can spin a man around
or that dreamy obliviousness you always see
in the blissed-out eyes of the just-fallen?
However they managed to round them all up,
one thing's for certain: the molecule is short-lived.
The published results (in *Psychoneuroendoctrinology*)
show conclusively that falling in love triggers
a fantastic jump in the level of NGF of new lovers,
but only for a brief time, and never for more than a year.
The fire consumes itself and the passion vanishes
like smoke in the wind in the hills of Tuscany.
The quantity of the love molecule in the blood falls
back to normal, where it hovers for the rest of us,
as we mope through our days and nights hoping
against hope to be one of the lucky ones
chosen for the very next experiment.

Super Sex Breakthrough

HEY, LOVER, YOUR PENIS IS SHRINKING,
says the headline in the Sunday paper's supplement.
Great, I think, just what I want to hear as I approach sixty,
but it's a fact — French urologists have found that penis volume
actually shrinks nearly 25% from age 30 to 80!
The fine print suggests a relationship between high cholesterol
and the disappearing penis, so I'm double-doomed.
Not only will my heart explode before I'm well into my 60s,
but my penis will noticeably shrivel up beforehand.

So Freud was wrong after all —
most sexual problems are not in the mind!
What was I afraid of, then, all those complicated years,
anxious about every encounter with every girl I met,
a walking example of psycho-sexual dysfunction,
suspicious of every pleasant pelvic tingle I'd ever imagined?
After all I had a full-sized penis.

Is there no hope? Is there nothing that can be done?
Yes, yes, there is! I'm amazed to read on.
Researchers at the Institute of Sexology in Paris
have found a way to nip my problem in the bud:
they've put *yohimbe,* Nature's most powerful aphrodisiac,
along with other drugs, into a formula called Testerex.
For only $29.95, I can get a 30-day supply of this magic potion
that increases my sexual desire, lowers my cholesterol,
boosts my energy and endurance, balances my blood pressure,
fights against aging, and actually enlarges my penis.

I am tempted, sorely tempted, to give this Testerex a try.
Such a small price to pay — don't you think? —
for safe and risk-free enhanced sexual performance,
and, at the very least, a hedge against shrinkage.

Metaphors

I want to be perfectly clear
right from the beginning
that I am speaking quite literally —
metaphors are dangerous.
We all suspect that, especially
when love is at the heart
of the matter.

This is a true story. The package
arrived wrapped in brown paper
but he knew the handwriting
— it was his ex-girlfriend's —
and the card taped crookedly
to the outside simply said
Beware of the live grenade inside,
and that's all it took:

cruisers cordoned off the avenue,
bomb-sniffing dogs circled
the plain brown box as if
it were a glittering Taj Mahal
made of the purest cocaine
until at last after meticulously
probing every inch of that box
the bomb squad determined
there were no explosives there.

Meanwhile the ex-girlfriend
had been arrested, taken down
to the station for questioning.

She insisted it was all a big
misunderstanding, a dark joke:
"I was using *grenade* as a metaphor,"
she told the befuddled officers
who booked her nonetheless
for *playing with fire* and other
assorted crimes of the reckless heart.

By now we should all know love
is a minefield and metaphors
are its weapons.

Romance in the Days before E-mail

Everyone knows romance
lives in expectancies, blooms
in the hours and days of waiting
for the next chance meeting,
for the slow sensuous morphing
of touch into kiss, of braided
fingers into the dazzle of lips
before all breathing stops and
the heart begins its new life.

This kind of love takes time
to grow, feeds on doubts and
indecisions, lives in daydreams
of imagined pleasures, a history
of desire that simply can not
be written in instant messages.
Romance needs the tectonics
of time shifting all around it,
needs distance and anxiety.

Three months into marriage
my father spent a lunch hour
writing a letter to my mother.
My dearest wife, he began,
still too shy even to name her,
*every day I pray to become
more worthy of your love.*
He posted that letter in a box
and waited three days for

his feelings to climb ten miles
of crooked streets from Pittsburgh
to Mt. Troy, every night looking
into her eyes, imagining her
reading his tender words
while during the days he sketched
his plans at the drafting table.
Three whole days when his life hung
in the balance of romance.

On Living in a City Not Far from the Zoo

Afterwards it felt so good to fall
asleep together on that four-poster bed,

the tall windows all wide open,
branches drooping in the humid air,

our breathing starting to settle
seamlessly into comfortable rhythms,

thinking now maybe of the children
curled up on cool sheets in their rooms,

the city's sirens suddenly silenced
by the weave of night's invisible truce.

Then just before sweet oblivion,
the wind-up would begin, eerie voices

screaming through the forests,
insistent, sharp cries of the jungle —

orangutans, two of them, the rising
pitch, the throaty song of chase

and capture, the ancient purpose,
the mirror of our deeper dream.

Making the Bed

It was time to change the sheets again.
She'd tossed the crumpled ones

on the floor by the door, then vanished,
so I began the stupid job alone,

maneuvering the prodigious mattress
all around the awkward frame,

stretching the fitted bottom to reach
the impossibly distant corners,

smoothing the wrinkles up on top
with a silky slide of my palm,

fingers and eyes moving in concert
until at last all that was left was

to arrange the pillows and drape
the comforter over the bed,

the daylight now slipping through
the feckless curtains, dream

and desire almost gone, everything
so trim I'd all but given up and

then she called my name and then
we unmade that bed for hours.

Captivated

That's what they called it
     — all of them — in sermons

and stories, in broadsides
     and diaries, letters to kinfolk,

sometimes even scrawled
     in haste on the bark of trees:

a little girl only seven yr.
     captivated by the Indians,

stolen away from the flames
     in the company of mothers

and babies, and maybe a few
     scared older boys and girls.

And so began the only
     cross-cultural experience

available to the Americans,
     everyone on the other side

of the divide, it seems,
     wanting desperately now

to know just how savage
     were the savages, how naked

would those captives become,
      how dense were those forests,

how seductive was the touch
      of red skin, the lure of barbaric

whispers, the aura of their fires,
      the freedom of the wilderness.

Michael Cervas lives with his wife Deb on the campus of Westminster School in Simsbury, Connecticut. From his backyard, he can watch the sun rise over Talcott Mountain and the Farmington River thread its way through the valley below. It is a perfect place for reading and writing. At Westminster, Michael teaches English and directs the school's Poetry Festival as well as the Readings in the Gund Room series. He also enjoys playing music (especially jazz) and sports (especially squash), both of which he considers simply to be other forms of poetry. *Captivated* is his second book of poems.

This book is set in Garamond Premier Pro, which had its genesis in 1988 when type-designer Robert Slimbach visited the Plantin-Moretus Museum in Antwerp, Belgium, to study its collection of Claude Garamond's metal punches and typefaces. During the mid-fifteen hundreds, Garamond—a Parisian punch-cutter—produced a refined array of book types that combined an unprecedented degree of balance and elegance, for centuries standing as the pinnacle of beauty and practicality in type-founding. Slimbach has created an entirely new interpretation based on Garamond's designs and on comparable italics cut by Robert Granjon, Garamond's contemporary.

To order additional copies of this book
or other Antrim House titles, contact the publisher at

Antrim House
21 Goodrich Rd., Simsbury, CT 06070
860.217.0023, AntrimHouse@comcast.net
or the house website (www.AntrimHouseBooks.com).

•

On the house website
are sample poems, upcoming events,
and a "seminar room" featuring supplemental biography,
notes, images, poems, reviews, and
writing suggestions.